"*Every now and then,* you run into a book that takes you to *another place*! The author takes you on a journey that allows the reader to see vivid pictures through her words, laughter and experiences!

Although a true story,
about the darkness she experienced amid her neglect and the shame of *many* traumas -

***THIS book* SWINGS!**

&

THIS book *DANCES!*"

Yvette Searson, CEO
Mental Health Training Solutions

I Have Something to Say:

I Said It!

Book One

of a

Three-Part Journey

By

TABITHA

BROGDON,

Daughter, Mother, Entrepreneur and Preacher…
Business Consultant, Accountability Coach,
Trainer, and Speaker

*BUT **YOU** CAN CALL ME **FRIEND***

. . . .

Requests for information should be addressed to:
TabithaBrogdon1@gmail.com

Visit us to Learn More and/or for Product Purchases:
www.tabithabrogdon.com

Cover Design by:
Eric Tobin

Cover Photo: **rawpixel®**

Printed in the USA **ISBN 978-0-578-48500-3**

DEDICATIONS

*I give God glory for seeing me strong enough to endure this journey He placed me on, and courageous enough to share it with the world, for what I believe to be '**such a time as this**.'*

I can fully exhale today because I had something to say…, and ***I SAID IT!***

To My Daddy & Mommy– Who loved me enough to conceive and birth me and are my biggest supporters…

To My Stepmom– Who loved us all like her blood ran thru our veins…

To My Previous Stepdads– Who parented children they did not seed…

To My (6) Caregivers & Foster Parents– Who made room in their homes, in their lives, and in their hearts for me…

To My Family & Siblings (blood, step, & foster)– Who have allowed me to be mom, big sister, friend, confidante, and 'just Tab'…

To the Mayewood High School Vikings– My place of balance and refuge from the storm…

To My Pastor, 1st Lady, and NMCC Family– Who loved me faithfully…

To My ride/die Big Sisters, Big Brothers, and Friends– Who put up with me (*as I put up with them* **lolol**!); and to **another one of my Big Sisters-** who edited this book for me…

To All - Thank you!

And to my sons – my heartbeats,
that kept me going:
Eric Alexander, Christopher, & V'ladell
Sons…, for giving me your blessings and
support to share my life– a life that is
extremely 'colorful'
with the world,

"Thank you." -Mom

SPECIAL RECOGNITIONS – PART1

To My Pre-Paid book order Supporters *that thought it not robbery to invest in me and the vision God gave me, in a book, you had* ***yet*** *to read… (****WOW****) -* ***Thank you!***

Listed in Order by Purchase:

St. Vick
Marlean Dozier-Smith
Hermeione Davis
E'Shann Wright
Julia Jackson
LeAnder Harvey
Eric McCray
Kenneth Bell
Felicia Greene
Natilus Thornton
Anthony Thompson
Lori Thompson
Phyllis Russell
Ruby Parker
Jacqueline Turner
James Richardson
Edward Brogdon
Thomas Fullard
Aleashia Conyers
Yvette Searson
Bobbie Bones-Byrd
Jacob Bedford

Special Recognitions – PART2

To My Pre-Paid book order Supporters** that thought it not robbery to invest in me and the vision God gave me, in a book, you had **yet** to read… (**WOW**) - **Thank you!

Listed in Order by Purchase:

Doris Glover
Darlene Sanders
Renea Pierre
Lori Smith
LaCresha Chatman
Cherilyn Chatman
Gloria Sanders
Harley/Rembert Fmly
Deborah Patterson
Hardeman/Evans Fmly
Lou Ester Brown
LaDonna Roberts
Tracy Reed
Angela Tyus
Wayne Tyus
Adam Wash
Kathy Hodges
Natalie Morman
James Thornton, III
Brenda Usher
Joshua Peltier

CONTENTS . . . . PART 1

CONTENTS . . . . PART 2

CONTENTS . . . . PART 3

I HAVE SOMETHING TO SAY:

I SAID IT!

PART ONE

"I ain't Embarrassed, nor am I Apologizing for Saying it the Way I Feel It"

. . . .

Disclaimer & Introduction

Let's get a **few** things straight right out the gate:

1. I **am** educated.
2. I understand grammar and punctuation **quite well**, but,
3. If you will allow me to *express it,* **how I feel it**... you will see that **I <u>have</u> something to say**!

In addition, I forewarn you, **you are gonna have to** (yep..., **'gonna have to') I see you** – *fix ya face, chiile!*) **LOL**

You are gonna have to keep up with me, honey! ... I've been holding this stuff in for a

veeeery long time…! Let's *laugh together*. Let's *cry together*. Let's take '**a** ***Journey***'!

But **first…**, let me go ahead and tell you my secret….

Secret??

Yes. I kept a secret, for 11 months and 6 days, that I was living alone with my 7-year old and 11-month old siblings. We were abandoned. I was 15-years old... didn't know what to do or who to tell…

What!! *How did you!?! – I mean,* ***what did you****...* ***GIRL****, you don't* ***look like****…!*

I know. (sigh)

Let me start from the beginning…

Once upon a time

Really!

Hold up, now! This is some **deep** stuff I am about to share. Let me get my nerves together! **Geesh**… ain't you an inquiring mind! **LOL**

(Deep breath … Blow it out… Breathe, Tabitha breathe …) Okay! You got this! **Let's go!** - *And no more interrupting please.* **LOL**

Once upon a time, this beautiful, **lovely**, **pecan**-chocolate girl entered the world via the city of Great Falls, Montana.

Yes! There ARE black people in Montana! I tell folks there are *about 4,* and I left, **so now there are 3**! **lololol**!

Anyways, this girl was **me** –

'Tabitha Brogdon.'

There is only one thing I *really*

remember about Montana. **THE AIR!**

Imagine the **coooooldest** day you have ever experienced; and you step outside, with a **mint** in your mouth, and then you **inhale**!

Mannnnn, that air was just **CRISP**!

I don't recall experiencing **'air' like THIS** annnnnnnny other place!

It was just... ***"CRISP**!!"*

I remember we moved around a lot too. From Montana to Wyoming, - **yep! Just 4 black people there as well** (just joking – **there were 5!) lololol**

Then we moved to North Carolina –

Seymour Johnson, Air Force Base.

Niiiiiiiiiiiicest people ever!

There is something special

***about the Carolinas**…,*

*North **and** South…*

'In the Beginning'
There *were* Parents

. . . .

Now of course, before me, ***there were parents!*** **LOL.** My daddy, who is also pecan-chocolate …

Pecan-chocolate???

Yaaaas, chiiiile! – We come in **ALL SHADES** of blackness! **LOL**

Daddy was in the Air Force and my mommy – she was more of a *vanilla bean*. Mommy **is** black – but southerners would call her '**high yellow'** … **'red boned'...**

And ***hoooonae***!

Now you TALKIN' bout, call her THAT – boy, that will get you STRAIGHT cussed out! (**Humph**! Shaking my head and **scared** to **LOL**!)

OH! - In case you didn't know "**lol**" means laugh / laughing out loud…
(I'm s*avin' you a Google-it honey!) "LOL"*

Mommy could not STAND those racist remarks… She taught us to love **everyone** - ***Black, white, green, or purple!***

Anyways, my mommy was a Registered Nurse. I do not remember ***when*** my parents divorced…

I just remember one day... daddy was gone.

Now **here** is where the ride is *about to get bumpy,* so **buckle up** and **hold on, my friend**!

Mommy, Stepdad #1, Sister #1, and My Introduction to Child Support: *It wasn't pretty!*

. . . .

I remember by the time we were in North Carolina, I was about 7-years old. I had Stepdad #1 and a new baby sister (Sister #1) on the way.

Okay – Sister #1??

Yes honey! **"I"** have something to say – I didn't say **SHE** did! **LOL -** Plus, it takes a lot of courage to tell you about **my** journey…, So **nope**, no names boo!

Stay focused now or you're gonna get lost in the sauce!

… Now Stepdad #1 was amaaaaaazing to me! I wanted to call him dad. I DID call him dad…, but just one time. CAN YOU SAY: "**Bad mistake**…." (SMH)

Chiiiiiile, I called Stepdad #1 'dad' one time and my mommy went **OFF**! **"That ain't your daddy!" - - Huuuuh?!?**

I'm like **geeesh** lady, I know that. (**Of course** in my inner voice – *"no **need** to get **cussed out**!"*)

Why did you marry him if I can't call him daddy?

And where is my daddy at anyway!?!

Ohhhhhhh, *to be caught in the middle of something* ***you did not create!***

Divorce is a **beast**...for **evvvveryone** involved!

But so is marrying **the wrong person** in the first place, **or for the wrong reasons,**

or if you **ain't ready**

– ain't healed –

JUST ***DON'T DO IT***

IF YOU **'AIN'T'**!

Anywhooooo..., Stepdad #1 was good to us. **Howsahnevah** – he was no saint (...well, he **WAS**, *but you know what I mean!)* **lololol**

I **loved** that man, but **hoooooney**..., **let me tell ya**!!!

I remember once mommy didn't get her **full** income tax return because he was behind on child support... for some child**SSS** (yes, I **should** say 'children') but some child**<u>SSS</u>**, **multiple** one's honey!!!) that MY MAMA **didn't** birth **or** know anything about!

Bae-Bae!

Ohhhhhhhhhhh, that chick set it double-down **OFF**!! **LOLOLOLOL**!!!!

YES! Oh Yes, she did!

And <u>THAT</u>

was my introduction to 'Child Support'!

It wasn't pretty!

It wasn't pretty at 'tal! … **lololol** *and shaking my head… Ummph, ummph , UMMPH* !! ….

And that's **ALLLL** I got to say about that!

LOL

Mommy, Sister #1, and 'this dude'

He told us EXACTLY who he was the 1ST time we met him: My Introduction to Domestic Violence

. . . .

So now we have left North Carolina,

and we moved to South Carolina ...

Stepdad #1 is gone. **Another** divorce honey...

And along comes **this dude**.

This dude was **MEAN**!

He was **ALWAYS** angry.

He was *always* **DRUNK.**

Mommy worked so **haaaaaaaard**

to make him happy. (sigh)

I tell you…

I remember mommy crying a **lot**.

I remember sitting on the couch shaking, as I listened to him do **things** to her in the other room…

She **screamed! -** He laughed.

She cried... - I cried.

I remember her telling me she was going to fix it.

I remember us trying to run away one time.

I remember him chasing us off the highway.

We almost wrecked! But we got away… for a while.

But then the **stalking** began after we **fiiiiiiiinally** found somewhere else to stay!

I remember the night he found us… He broke in and tore up our house. The cops came. They promised they would arrest him… they **promised.**

I heard them promise!

But I remember him showing **back** up to our house… **Busting** through the front door… **dragging** her down the hallway *by her hair…*

punching her…

kicking her…

stomping her…!

cussing her…!

I remember there was nothing else I could do.

No house phone, no police!

I tried to help her fight – but he was so **big**…

He was **sooooo damn BIG**!

That was a **very** bad night…

I remember.

I was not surprised at how this ended…

He told us EXACTLY WHO HE WAS, the 1ST time we met him…

Why didn't mommy believe me?

I was not acting out.

I was not trying to make her *choose*.

I just knew she deserved to be treated better than this.

I just loved her…

I wish I could undo **what I saw**, and ***what I heard***…

I wish she had not gone on the second date, **because it led to a third, and a forth…!**

I wish she loved herself enough to know she deserved better.

I wish my love for her were enough versus her need to be loved any type of way…

That was NOT love!

That was **abuse**!

That was wrong!

And I wish he would have realized how badly he made her feel!

I wish he would have gotten help!

I wish he did not drink like that - He was a *little* nicer when he was not drunk and high. *Just a little…*

Why didn't **he** see this?

Why didn't he see **US**!?!

We were kids!

Whhhhhhhhy didn't he get help?

Why didn't he STOP?

Mommy, Sister #1, Stepdad #2 and Brother #1
SURELY things are About to Get Better

. . . .

We got away from 'this dude' **somehow**. Not sure of the space in time, but now we are with a new man – Stepdad #2. Annnnnnd shortly after, my new baby brother (Brother #1) was born. **YES**! **Now** I have **two** siblings! **SURELY things are about to get better!** *A new man = a family.*

...I did not understand back then that you did not HAVE to have both parents in the home to be an 'official family...'

– I know now. *But my mindset then,* was **now** we can get back to <u>love</u>!

Love?!?

That was a funky beginning!

You moved from state to state…

You had no dad…

Then you ***get*** *a* ***new dad****, but you* ***cannot call him dad****…!*

TWO *divorces!*

The ***abuser*** *dude!*

Then another ***Stepdad***

Love?!?

Yes chiiiile, **LOVE**!!

It was not bad all the time!

I could *easily* only remember
the bad stuff…
Somehow,
I learned at an early age,
how to hold on ***TIGHT***
to the good stuff, too!

Let me tell ya some of the

other things

that I remember!

I HAVE SOMETHING

TO SAY:

I SAID IT!

PART TWO

Flashback – *It wasn't ALL Bad:* *'Our Family Traditions'*

. . . .

Every dinner we had a **FULL** meal **with** a **home cooked** dessert, honey!! Peach cobbler! Blackberry cobbler! Banana Pudding, and them four-layered Strawberry cakes! Oh, my mommy could **BUUUUUUURN,** chile!

Smothered pork chops!

Fried chicken!

Cornish hens (Yes **'Cornish'** … **we were bougie, chile**!) **lololol**

Liver and onions (**Oh don't play!)** With the **gravy** over some **Mahatma** White rice – **Shut the front door**! -Oooooou-**wee**!!

Okra and tomatoes with thin cut pork-chops…!! With some sweet **Jiffy** corn bread on the side! BaeBEE! - We ate **good**!

And **Special Days** - **Shooooot**!

My birthdays with mommy were **ALWAYS** amazing!

And **Christmas**! - Mannnnnnnnnn, we would sit around the Christmas tree and watch the lights that were **sooooo** pretty!

OH! - And I remember dancing all night to **Motown**! - "Silent Night"… "Santa Claus is Coming to town"… "I saw Mommy Kissing Santa Claus" – **REAL** holiday music!

The house… the decorations… the smell of holiday food – and *of course* we made "cookies and left out that glass of milk"…!

But the **magic** was **in the morning**! **Neeeeeever** was rushed off to bed Christmas eve. Some years, we stayed up until 2am… But it never failed!

When we woke up!

On *Christmas morning*!

MAAAAAAAGIC!

The house looked like a Toy Store!

Stuff all **OVER** the place!

And I **looooooooove me some** Charlie Brown Christmas!

To **this day**,

I watch it every year... and I make my sons watch it with me... even though they are adults. **LOLOL**!

I have told them

(Alex, Chris, and V'ladell) -
"Whenever y'all have kids,

my grandbabies ***bettah***

watch Charlie Brown Christmas!"

(And now my request is official)

***– I have put it in 'published' writing*!**

Don't Play!

LOL

Flashback – *Are you READY TO LAUGH??!!!???*
Almost
Dr. Tabitha L. Brogdon: 'Trauma Queen'

. . . .

I remember in the 2nd grade getting all A's. My reward was a white canopy bedroom set, with *Strawberry Shortcake décor,* honey! But those A's backfired - Chiiiiile! - let me tell ya! **I just KNEW** I was going to be ***a Trauma Surgeon*** … **because my mommy told me so! lololol**

"Since you're a Straight A student you will be a doctor – a surgeon

– and you'll make loooooots of money!"

From 7-years old, thru college, to taking Medical exams, to graduation, **I just KNEW** I was going to be working in the ER honey!

And then my husband –

Well my Ex-husband #1 ….

Your Ex-husband #1 ??

What?!?

Fix ya face, chiile - That is another book – **stay focused!**

My Ex-husband #1 gets this boil on his thigh. We **both** are going to school to go medical, so we **both** go into the Emergency room!

I got this! - It's **just** a boil!

…**Baaaaaaaaaaaaaae-bae!**

I remember that doctor running a scalpel thru that bad boy! I remember grey **puss** and **runny stuff** oooooooooozing down his thigh! (**RIGHT**!!) - **I see you** – *fix ya face, chiile!* **Lol** And, I remember **no more**!

BAM!

Your girl was **OUT**!!

On the floor!! - Night-Night, Irene!

Almost **Dr. Tabitha L. Brogdon,**

The Trauma Queen!

Mannnnnnnnnnnn, in that moment, this **pre-med-last-year-of-college-aint-no-way-in-HeeeeLL-we-doing-this!**-chick was like:
Oh! **My**! **GOD**! - **Whhhhy** did I go to school for this???

Oh yeah – …

My mommy told me, since I was a Straight A student that I could be a doctor

"a surgeon –

and I'd make loooooots of money!"

Honey chile, uh, *Noooooooooo!*

I don't do **ANNNNNNN-NEEY-THING**

that **drips**,

oozes,

snots,

or runs,

orrr bleeds!

Your girl ain't NEVAH (NEVAH-evah-evah!) even pulled **a tooth** out of her 3 children's mouth! … It's **loose**….???

When you go to school, ask your teacher to please pull it out for you.

She **won't** mind!

You want the tooth out or not!?!

LOLOL

Follow your PASSION!!
NOT A DOLLAR bill!

Dollar chasing will have you somewhere you DON'T want to be!

(IJS) … "I'm Just Sayin!"
(I saved ya another *Google-it,* honey!)
LOL

Flashback-
Words DO sometimes hurt me

. . . .

I also remember being called

"a princess." I was mommy's "**princess**."

I remember asking her why **I** couldn't be a queen. She said, "Cause I'm the damn queen!" **(lololol... actually - I am hollering and lol!!!)** Sounds mean, but thinking back now, it was funny as heck! Gotta love it! She **always** shot the arrow straight! That was her way of loving.

She wasn't a hugger though..., but gave me lots of affirmation– "Princess, you are smart..." ... "Princess, you're pretty ..."

"Yes, you are my lil princess, ***but don't drink coffee... - it'll make you black."***

What the ...!

*Don't do **what**?!??!*

***Black... what's wrong with being black**?!?*

Did I **ask** her what was wrong with... (**Uh – Nooooo!** I done told y'all - *"No **need** to get **cussed out**!")*

However, ... I internalized those words... for **years**. She was not **only** the queen – but also the **vanilla, light-skinned** queen...

...and me – "a **chocolate** *princess..."*

I could not ever be a queen, I thought, –

because "I" was **dark-skinned**.

I am sure she did not mean that.

Mommy loved me.

However…, some of the words,

no matter how it *may **not** have been meant,*

still created a voice in my mind,

that took **years** to silence……………………

I am mindful of **the power** of <u>words</u>.

I am mindful that **words**
can **build** *Kings* and *Queens*.

I am also mindful that words
can **break identities**
and **cremate**
innocent
souls.

I am mindful that
Sticks and Stones
May or may not
<u>ever</u>
break my bones,

But WORDS

<u>DO</u>

Sometimes
hurt
me.

Mommy said when I got older, I needed to marry a man with **a job**, **a car**, and **good shoes**...*She never mentioned to marry a man that loved me...*

Mommy said we were not going to church cause' church folks were nothing but a bunch of hypocrites... **lololol**!!! – (**Now, I ain't throwin' no shade**, because you know ya gurl **loves** the Lord...), but **lololol**... well.... I'll leave that alone for now...

So... *how did ya girl handle all of this?* - **Chiiiiiile**, I stayed **out** of church, grew up and found me a **workin'**, **4-door driving**, **Nike wearing** brutha and I stayed **faaaaaaaaaaar** AWAY from the Folgers coffee! **Lololol**

But that was childhood – *at least what I remember.*

FLASHBACK memories will SHO-NUFF make you put life into perspective.

If I were a kid again,
I would not rush through 'the good stuff'!

I *would not RUSH*
to be ***grown***.

I *would not RUSH*
to get to the ***next thing*** –

NO -
I would taaaaaaake my **tiiiiime**…
and **embrace** <u>**each**</u> day…,

and

EVERY

_moment.

If I were a kid again, I would have **laughed** *harder*!

I would have said **thank you** *more*!

I would have *looked people in the eye and <u>put in extra effort</u> "to see them!"*
(Because what I later learned,
the most difficult way I could ever imagine) was,

you **<u>never</u>** know when **'this look'** will be the **'last look'** ...

Oooooh, if I were a kid again
I would have practiced

BEING
IN
THE MOMENT

So ... , back to *South* Carolina.

Flashback – *That House on Radical Road*

. . . .

There is Mommy, ***Stepdad #2, Sister #1, & Brother #1*****: … and that house on** ***Radical Road.***

Ohhhhhh, if that house could talk **baeBEE** it would tell y'all **some thangs**!

…**That house** saw drugs. I had *never* been around cocaine…, until we moved into that house.

…**That house** heard arguments about **multiple** affairs… **you** didn't come home… **where were you**... I **followed** you… your family **this**… and your family **that**!

...That house saw the mental **breaking** of a woman that was **already** broken... **mommy used to smile... I thought things were about to get better**! At least that is what Stepdad #2 said! Is ***this*** better?!?

...**That house** saw a man that would not stay home and ***rarely*** spoke to any of us when he did.

...**That house** saw **kids** ... that were **always** nervous..., and sad..., but *afraid* to even **cry**!

...**That house** saw mommy wake up one day to tell me that an aunt in another state died and that she was leaving to take care of the funeral arrangements... ***But I knew of no family in that state***...

Mommy, why are you packing **evvverything** you can fit into your car?!? - Mommy, why aren't you packing any of **our** things? **Mommy**! **WHEN WILL YOU BE BACK**?!?

"Tab. You are the oldest. You are in charge. Take this envelope. Do NOT open it unless there is an emergency and you don't hear from me."

...**That house** watched my mommy, *with tears in her swollen eyes,* hug her 11-month old son for the last time, her 7-year old daughter, and me at age 15 – as she got in her car – saying over and over again,

"I love you, guys - please *remember*, I love you."

That house watched her drive away.

That house watched Stepdad #2 come and gather his stuff and leave as well. I don't know where he went. He just left.

That house…

on Radical Road… it kept **many** secrets…

It kept **my** secret.

For 11 months and 6 days, I lived alone with my 7-year old and 11-month old siblings.

We were abandoned. I was 15.

I didn't know what to do or who to tell.

Sister #1, Brother #1, and Me
Abandoned and Left with *"Strategy"*

. . . .

Strategy became my best friend!

Bill collectors called and I would get soooo nervous. **Strategy** said:

"We don't have time for fear!

DO WHAT YA

GOTTA DO!"

Soooo, - I lied to keep the utilities on.

(My mama put the check in the mail!)

I created that line! **(LOL)**

Newsflash... that **won't** work today!

Strategy said:

"YOU MUST **GO TO SCHOOL** AND

GET AN EDUCATION!

DO WHAT YA

GOTTA DO!"

So, I told the babysitter that mommy was working early shifts **and** late shifts … (sighing….) *the babysitter knew better,* ...but she watched the 11-month old **for free** so I could go to High School.

Your clothes don't fit! You must be broke! - -Ohhhhh, the kids that **bullied** and picked on me... Embarrassing! ... But they didn't know better... They were kids. And **FACTS**... my clothes **DIDN'T** fit and we **sho-nuff** was broke **(Laughing with tears)** **Strategy** said, "C**uss em' out!!' LOLOLOL**

Did I?? ... We'll talk about that a little later.

Stay focused! – **LOLOLOL**

I will say this:

I hate when people get bullied.
If bullies only knew the pain their actions really caused...

Let me also say that **I was not a fan of lying**. I was a fan of **survival.** . I did the best thing **I KNEW to do** at 15-YEARS OLD to survive…, and frankly… I did not have time to weigh in and seek approval.

People go through things that **are just HARD!**

AND **COMPLEX**! AND **SCARY**!

But at some point, we **all** must

figure something out.

When life hits you -

HIT BACK

AND HIT BACK **HARDER**!

When life gets *complex* - **break it down** into

bite-size pieces!

Figure out a way to make it *not so BIG,*

not so OVERWHELMING!

Create "Step 1"

- and **take it...!**

and "**Step 2**" – and **take i**t!

and "Step 3"! -**Annnnnd TAKE IT!**

And when life gets scary – **Brave up**!

Turn your fear into **STRATGEY** and

knock that joker OUT!!

Coping with Abandonment

. . . .

How did I cope? - **My alma mater – "Mayewood High"!** Mayewood High school – home of the mighty **Viii-KINGS**! **Whoop! Whoop! Whoop - Shout-out!!**

Don't *ever* forget where you come from homey! (Yes, "homey")
***Google-it* honey! LOLOL**

I **GOT** to show **some love**!

All the kids did not bully me. I had **more than a few** that were extremely KIND!

Mayewood Vikings: ***"Thank you for being my family! My refuge! I laughed with you MANY days because I had cried all night long the day before."***

But there, in the halls of the MIGHTY VIKINGS – I was a cheerleader, in the National Honor Society, in Journalism, in the Science club, and I stayed on the honor role – OH, I **worked** them grades honey! (Ain't no need to be abandoned *and dumb*, **at least not on purpose!)**
I mean, WHO DOES THAT??!!??

"And Mayewood, thanks for having the BEST Teachers and Coaches!"

I am convinced that we got the best education in the STATE there; and it is also there where I got the best therapy ever … Through laughter, through love, through friendships, annnnnd through writing.

Yes, **writing**! - *It was my therapy, Chile!*

I came across a poem I wrote in the 11th grade, called "**Alone**".

It pretty much captured how I felt when I left school each day…

ALONE

Left alone in this world.
Searching for a peace of mind.

Comparing my life to the 'other girls.'
While trying to leave the past behind.

I've questioned why things are how
they are.

I've wondered why I feel so sad.

And each night I pray upon a star,
for God to restore the happiness
I once had.

Bearing the hurt that I feel,
with teary eyes I try to move on.

Telling myself that the pain isn't real;
with hope, I face another dawn.

And as the sun rises
to begin another day,
like the dark night
my problems fade away.

Tabitha L. Brogdon

Two of my poems made it to the hands of Hillary Carlip, **an author** of a book called, *"Girl Power – Young Women Speak Out."* And that book made it on **Oprah Winfrey's Book Club list**, which made its way to **college campuses allll across the United States, and is still being sold today**!

Now hold on, honey! Close your mouth – your gurl did **NOT** blow up! **lololol** …

I got jacked, chile!

Let me tell you - your gurl was not ***even aware*** that her poems was in print until **25+ years later**!

But… what an honor to have my work published as an inspiring message to other young ladies. ***(And Hillary … you owe me some change boo!)*** IJS. **lololol**

You gotta **laugh**!

You know what I mean… LOL

I wrote about ***many*** things to cope..., but I never quite built up the courage to write about my "**Big Secret**"… Until now.

… I have something to say...:

MY BIG SECRET was that there was this senior that I confided in that I thought was a big brother to me. I remember the day I told him our situation… His response, however, I was **not** prepared for…

"If you do this ..., I'll bring y'all some food from Piggly Wiggly when I get off work."

Still makes me sad…

No LOL here, my friend.

So, what did I do?...

To feed my sister and brother... who I felt like were **my** kids..., I did "**this**"... and I did "**that**."

Humiliated.

He was 18 and **I was only 15**!

But, ...

they ate...

But then he graduated & moved... and the food ran out.

My 11-month old says,

"Mama (thought I was his mommy) ***I'm hungry."***

"TWO Ritz crackers."

(Tears… many, many tears)

That is all we had left.

So, I finally realized, THIS MUST BE THE EMERGENCY MOMMY was talking about… - so I opened the envelop that mommy left.

Funny…, as smart as I was, I have been asked a GAZILLION times, "*Why did you wait so long to open the envelop?*"

And I often wondered, Tab, why wasn't the emergency "your mommy has left, and it has been 11 months"?!?

…I don't know.

But when my sister and brother started **crying** because they were **hungry,** and they had **nothing** left to eat… **THAT** was **my 9-1-1!**

And when I was a teen, I had 'Christians' say some of the meanest things about my parents, my circumstances, and the choices I made to feed my siblings – and then they would seal it with a 'Jesus-Stamped' scripture that, I would later discover, they ***TOTALLY*** *took out of context.* **SMH**

People ALWAYS HAVE A FREAKIN' opinion! - And I hate to say it, but sometimes especially in the church.

I don't think that they meant any harm, most of the times.

I just wish Chrisitians would THINK about some of the stuff they said before it came out their mouths! And for a little girl, that was not familiar with church, or the Bible, or Jesus –, I wish they would not make *their opinion,* His Scripture.

Like if you can't find it **in a Scripture**, maybe,

just **maaaaaaaaaaaaybe,**

<u>THIS</u>

is a time to **show compassion**

or just shut the **** up!

(Fix ya face - Calm down, honey!
Strategy cussed just now* - but I cleaned it up** *"*"***)**

People ALWAYS HAVE A FREAKIN' opinion about what someone else <u>should</u> have done *or* <u>should</u> <u>not</u> have done, espeeeeecially when they have no "dones" to pull from!

It would be interesting how much
healing could ***really*** take place
if people learned how to
speak in 'love'…
speak 'with compassion'…
and/or 'not speak at all',
if they can't find
the right words to say.

One of the things I will ***always*** *love about* ***Jesus****, and Christians* ***that are <u>intuned</u>****, is <u>they</u> <u>know</u> <u>what</u> to <u>speak</u>* … Luke 12:12
(Please Google-it, Honey!)

Anyways…

I will never forget when I opened that envelop

and read the letter.

Inside was a $100 bill and it read:

I (*my mommy's name*)

leave the care of my 3 children (*our names*)
to

this woman
(*who I never knew; and I wouldn't find out,*
***until 29 years later*).**

...The letter may have read something

else… That is just all I remember…

She was gone … *and she was not coming back.*

The senior was gone... *now there no more food.*

No more **help**.

No more...

I felt <u>cold</u>.

I felt like **bile** was coming up **through my very throat**.

I was too numb to cry. All I knew to do was **breathe**...

Strategy said to this 15-year old, baby girl:

You did *the best*

you knew to do.

It is ok.

<u>Don't</u> <u>beat</u> <u>yourself</u> <u>up</u>.

It's time…

"Ask for help."

Sooooo… I told an adult…, who would soon

become **Caregiver #1.**

It is OKAY to ask for help, especially when you don't know how to help yourself.

And here, my friend,

is where I gotta take a breather…

Woooooooh…

Again…if you will allow me to express it how I feel it… *this is a boo*k, **<u>but</u>** its **undressing**, and **unedited** <u>transparency</u> **all the way…**

It is here, where I hit "save" on my laptop, …

I MUST take a break!

There **is** a *happily ever after* at the end of this

Once upon a time….

I **promise**.

But we are not there yet.

….Lord, oh Lord…

I have said a lot - ***Lord,*** *I have said*

a ***<u>LOT</u>***.

Let's rest….

Day 1…. **rest**

Day 2… Okay, chiiiile –

I said it!

And I've got so much more to say… !

So, honey… l**et's do this!**

I HAVE SOMETHING

TO SAY:

I SAID IT!

PART THREE

Flashback – *'The Wink'* at The Club in Sauter's Town

. . . .

Caregiver #1 was one of my previous middle school teachers. Her house was the ONLY house before mommy left that I could go to for sleepovers… until **Sauter's Town** that is! **lololol**

Do I want to tell this story???

Aw-shucks! - I might as well!

LOL

Honey, Sauter's town was **this spot** out in the **cuuuuuuuuun-TREE** of the Carolinas! The last time I stayed over Caregiver #1's house (before mommy left) a little **sit-chu-a-shun** occurred…

The ladies' daughter (one of my best friends) and I snuck out to **the club**. (Oh yeah! **The spot** we went to was **a one way in, one way out CLUB** in Sauter's town!)

To this DAY, I loooooves me some hole in the wall clubs!

To this DAY??

Fix ya' face, honey… **I'm feelin' kinda judged!!** *Foooocus.* **LOLOL**

Let me tell ya! Let me tell ya! -

Mannnnnnnnnn, we were about 13-years old, in mini-skirts, and make-up'ed **down!**

We were CUTE, BRUH!!

Cute … ! - and **winking** our good **right** eye (**always** the right… the left doesn't get ya the same **magic**!)

You tried it just now didn't you! ***LOLOL*** *–* ***Go on and wink it, honey!! LOLOL***

Weeell **that wink** got us

thru the line outside!

And that wink got us

to the door!

Chiiiile, that wink got us

pass the bouncer, and IN THE BUILDING, without I.D.!

And that Magical wink even got us **on the dance floor**!

"All I want to do is zoom-a-zoom-zoom-zoom - And a poom-poom, just shake ya rump!" Wreckx-n-Effect

baeBEE!! - **Ya'll ain't ready!**

Oh, that was the JAM! -You bettah *Google-it*, Honey! LOLOL

Mannnnnnnnnnnnnnnn, we **shakin'** and **we winkin'**!

We **winkin'**!

And **we shakin'**!

Then **suddenly**!!!!

The lights come on!

The DJ <u>stops</u> the music!

And then "**THE ANNOUNCEMENT**"

was made…:

"Tabitha Loette Brogdon"

(YES!!!! - My government name, Chile!)

and Girl *(I won't give up her name lol),*

'Your mama is waiting at the door!'

What in the world!?!?

My Mama!!!!!!!!!!!?????????!!!!!!!!!!!!

Mannnnn, I looked at "the girl" and she

looked at me!

Frozen!

My feet said, "**You bettah go!**"

My behind said, "**UH-un!**"

Then I caught a glimpse of mommy at that door! Bruh! She had the **LOOOOOONGEST, BLAAAAAAAAAAACKEST**

BELT

I HAD EVER SEEN! - **Looked like a King Cobra snake!**

And **you know** how them old school mamas do! … She had that Cobra **wrapped** around the palm of her **RIGHT** hand – *(always the right!)* - **"THE RIGHT HAND" aka THE SWINGING HAND** – …with **juuuuust** enough belt left out for **leg wrapping**! Excuse my French…*but I wasn't saved back then… and if you will allow me to* ***express it*** *how* ***I felt it*** *….!* I was like **SHiiiiiiiiIT** – WHAT WE **NOT GON' DO**

IS GET A **BEATIN'**

IN **THE CLUB**!!!

I wasn't moving!

The girl (my friend) was scared…

"Tab, we got to **GO**!"

"SHUT UP!!", I said

"Girl, don't you see that snake in her hand!"

Family …..!

Let me tell ya'll!

It was then that I **learned** a lesson – about that "***magical wink***" – I was **NOT** the originator!

Nope!

Not mine!

I got that wink **from mommy**, but I didn't know it until ***this*** **moment that would follow**…

That chick (my mommy) was **staring** at me from the door! And I was **staring back** at her from the dance floor!

Jesus parted that club like a red sea!

But wasn't **NOBODY** movin'!

Wild, wild west Montana show-down…

*Oh, my GOD, I'm **NOT** gonna win!!*

Mannnnn, my mommy raised that **right** eyebrow *(always the **right**!)*

And then she put it on me!

"That Magical Wink!"

She **smiled**,...

WINKED

and

Exited the building!

That wink was **SILENT**, but it communicated **QUITE WELL**!

You see, my mommy was a Diane-Carroll-kindof-divah **(Today we call it bougie!)** **lololol –** and I knew **exaaaaaaaaaactly** what **that wink meant**! It meant,

"I am just as bougie as you are and I am not spanking you ***in the club****,...*

(YES! "spanking" - My mama was a spanker.... **Bougie** chile! **LOL**)

But ooooooh lil' girl, lil' ***girl****, ...**wait-til-you-get-your-a**-get-home!"***

(She was a cusser too) **LOLOL**

Bae! ...

I have said enough...!

...But what's interesting, now that I think about it today, she never beat me for that ... she put that **WINK on me**! *And that **was more than enough!*** And ... it was the **LAAAAAAAST TIME** that I could sleep over Caregiver #1's house, ...***of course. (smile)***

Old School Mamas
didn't yell
and they didn't scream,
and they **SHO-NUFF** wasn't sweating out
their **fresh roller-sets**!

They gave you '**the look'**, which was a
warning to go sat **(not sit)** –
NO - go **SAT** down somewhere!

And they gave you **'the wink'**, which meant,
not here…

and **not** now…

But we'll get up, shorty! Oh – We'll Get Up!

<u>**Straight**</u> **Gangstah**!

Oooooooh…
I love me
some School Mamas!

Before there were Foster Parents There were Caregivers

. . . .

But enough about that… the words I have always wanted to say to **Caregiver #1** were:

*"You were the first adult I told about being abandoned when we ran out of food. Thank you for taking Sister #1 and me into your home. (***Brother #1's dad took him to his family.****)*

Caregiver #1, thank you for never bombarding us with questions, but for just loving on us. Thank you for remembering we were children that had experienced trauma. Thank you for feeding us and not rationing out the portions.

You were not really a good cook, (lololol) <u>but you sure did serve what you cooked with love</u>! Thank you!"

Caregiver #1 let the Department of Social Services know. And that is when the bouncing from house to house began…

. . . .

Caregiver #2- She did not want us there…. We slept on the hardwood floors. No blanket. It was cold, *but it was a home*. She wanted babies, not a 7 and a 15-year old. I get it… I guess.

The Words I always wanted to say were:

"Caregiver #2, we really were not bad kids. We just had a bad situation. I am sorry for sneaking food. I wanted to make sure Sister #1 had food in case... in case... you ran out. It was my job to make sure she never ran out of food again! Although we were only with you for a few days, it was a few days we did not have to sleep on the street. Thank you for trying. <u>Thank you so much</u> for trying."

. . . .

When the caseworker picked us up from school, I already knew what that meant. Back to square one. And that is when we went to Caregiver #3.

Caregiver #3: Now **this lady** was the **BOMB.com!**

She housed me and Sister#1 for a couple of months! She taught us **soooooo** much! And she **loved** us so much! I have told her before, but not fully…

"Caregiver #3, thank you for buying us pretty clothes. It made the kids stop bullying me - for a while anyways. Lol

Your hugs <u>every night</u> before bed…, they were balm to my bleeding soul. And, thank you for teaching me speeches and giving me the courage to use my voice to inspire others! I had <u>NO</u> IDEA one day I would be a <u>teacher</u> to High School students! –

NO IDEA one day I would be a trainer in Corporate America! Caregiver #3, I had NO IDEA that one day, I would use my voice to teach and preach the Gospel! ... I wish we could have stayed longer with you. You treated Sister #1 and I like we were yours."

What I have **always** been mindful of,

especially now that I am an adult,

Is that you do not have to always verbalize your feelings.

Kids ***know***
when you love them...,

And *they* ***know***
when you don't...

Love is a **pooowerful** thing.

A Product of *the Good Side* of Foster Care

. . . .

We left the last Caregiver and went to Foster Parent #1. She provided everything we needed **financially**…like **clothes and hair appointments -** which was **soooo** special to me! *Before my mommy left, we got our hair done every day at home and every Friday at the salon.* Mommy loved us… **the best she knew how**… (Smile).

Foster Parent #1, I never had the courage to speak openly to you. I did not know how to express my feelings without it appearing like I was ungrateful.

Today, I have that courage.

"Foster Parent #1..., thank you for pushing me to get an education. Thank you for fighting to try to keep Sister #1 and I together. I know you were there..., but when her dad came and took her away, I died inside. You were an awesome provider. I just wished you weren't so tough. Tough love is necessary in life..., I get it. But sometimes your love hurt..., especially when I was just trying to heal."

Foster Parent #1 Took me to a counselor one time.

Yasssss, honey!

I broke the **Black-Folks-Ain't-Crazy** rule and went to a shrink!

LOLOL!!

"Counsel P".

She could not get me to talk.

I had no words to say…

And finally, one session – Fight came back for me! STRATEGY, SAID: "**GUUUUURL,**

I WAS DELAYED GETTING HERE,

BUT I'M BACK!"

Strategy and I had a **loooong** conversation.

*"I was going to have to keep coming here, **week after week, sitting in silence**, mad <u>**and**</u> sad **IF I KEPT CHOOSING NOT TO DO THE WORK!"***

Strategy said,

"Bae-BEE!!, Wipe those tears! Get over it! Get thru it! Get around it! DOOO SOMETHING!!!"

And I was **100%** on-board!

My New Mindset:

I will NOT stay broken!

"HOW DO WE DO THIS, doc???", I asked Counselor P.

I remember her smiling…

and giving me a signed Alice Walker book *(In search of our Mothers' Gardens).*

Within the insert I found Hope.

Counsel P wrote words that I will

NEVER,

EVER forget…, and that

20+ years later I am still able to flip to and read today.

She wrote:

"Life is a lot like the yellow brick road.

It's hard, firm, changing, sure, solid, full of wonderment and sometimes presents itself with occasional cracks.

You, Ms. Tabitha, are well on your way to learning how to step strongly over them to reach your goal.

Remember:

For women to make it,
the strong must survive,
and know that it takes
"each one to reach one"
and <u>you</u> are "one."

Counselor P - June 4, 1993

Mannnnnn, what did that lady tell me that for! Chiillle, I knew from that moment on, I had to get my power back!

***STRATEGY! COME ON - WE'VE GOT WORK TO DO!!**

I was still with Foster Parent #1. But one day, I got to the place where I could no longer handle lacking what I needed from her. I deserved more than a roof over my head…, food in my belly… and **stern** conversations. I deserved an opportunity **to live**.

So, I ran away.

"Foster Parent #1 – I still thank you. I ran away so I could have a fresh start. Thank you for alllllll that you did. You loved the best way you knew how. I believe that. And it was not wrong - it just was not right for me."

. . . .

I would rather take a chance on learning

how to love me and failing,

than successfully being loved incorrectly by someone else.

. . . .

Grand-daddy Willie Brogdon, ***deceased,*** **but his legacy lives on.** Why do I list HIS name? Good question. *I don't have an answer. I just know that it is necessary…*

Grand-daddy (Caregiver #4) housed me for a few days after I ran away. *What is funny is I had never seen a picture of my daddy up until this point.* I could not remember how he looked.

When I went into Foster Care, I never knew what happened to the things we had… But Grand-daddy had photo albums **gaaaauh-lore** – (**and, oh I was CUTE, Chil**e – *just as I had imagined!*) **LOLOLOL**!

Hoooooney, I cried **half the night**, flipping thru **pages** *after* **pages** of ME and MY DADDY when I was a little girl before he and mommy divorced.

Ohhh, and the land Grand-daddy lived on…that land was **on a street called** "**BROGDON** ROAD"! **Shut-the-front-door!** He had prop-per-tee, chile! And farm land, … And I remember a house in the back for family**!**

Grand-daddy was a BOSS honey! A straight up entrepreneur!

The State would not let me stay with Grand-daddy...

(Yaaaas, chile, they tracked your girl down like she was a fugitive!) ***LOLOLOL***

But by this time, I was a different chick! I had found the secret to my survival..., it was my mother's wit and my daddy's **Brogdon-blood**.

I knew at that very moment, that no matter **where** the State placed me, I was from that point, now and forevermore, **The Boss of Me!**

In order to successfully map out where I was going,

I needed to, at best possible, understand where I came from.

And even though it hurts sometimes, it still helped to know

"THE TRUTH".

When the State picked me up from Grand-daddy's house, they placed me with Foster Parent #2.

> Foster Parent #1 would not allow me to get my things I left at her home.
>
> I get it. She was hurt - upset that I ran away. She later did return my clothes… lol, but

by then I was in my final year of college, married, and about 8 months pregnant. (smh)…,

But any-who…

. . . .

Foster Parent #2 came with an **ARMY** of supplies. She had adult sons and an adult daughter. She had grandchildren. She had other foster children (There was 7 of us).

She too, was a business owner, and **baeBEE**, she walked **HEAVY** in **LOVE**!

I remember the first day I went to meet her. **Mannnnnnnnnnnnn**, you ain't **had a HUG** until you've been in her arms!

That lady hugged me **tight**! Hugged me **close**!

And I will never forget her words,

"Tabitha, welcome home!"

The **whole** family came together and made sure I had clothes to go back to college in! And her daughter would always remind me:

WE ALWAYS HAVE

A CHOICE.

THAT

IS WHAT LIFE IS ABOUT –

MAKING CHOICES…

GOOD CHOICES!

I loved her soooo much for these words!

Never forgot them!

I think her daughter, my big sister (lol) is a cousin of Strategy!

I call her sister because there was no term of 'foster' in this home.

I was treated like a family member.

No words of ill-will about my parents.

As a matter of fact, Foster Parent #2's exact words were, **Tabitha:**

"You never know what causes some people ***to do what they do or what keeps them from being as strong as we would like for them to be.***

But you got to learn how to forgive them all.

That's how God wants us to handle it.

And remember,

DON'T YOU EVAH

TAKE NO SHIT

OFF NO BODY!"

Yaaaaas, chile, this woman of God was the ***TRUTH****!* Humph! Be religious if ya want! –

I had **turned every cheek** I knew to turn, from my **jawbone** to my **tailbone**.

I was tired of being a victim!

And with a Christian cheerleader encouraging me to **FORGIVE** so **<u>I could LIVE,</u>** I now became a **<u>FORCE</u>** to be reckoned with!!

. . . .

I remained in Foster Care until I graduated college.

In 1996, I graduated from Morris College, <u>in Sumter, SC</u> **NOT** *as a doctor* lol, but in 3 years, because I went year-round.

I found **every family member** that I was separated from.... **Each and every one**.

And, today, I can say, by the grace of God, we are healing. **But <u>only</u> because we have put in, and *are still putting* in, a <u>lot</u> of WORK to do so.**

Fast forward to present day, in 2019, I have worked in **Corporate America in Human Resources for 20+ years**; have 3 ***amazing*** sons; and have birthed **2 beautiful businesses.** *One,* Executive Planning Solutions *that focuses on Leadership Development from a business perspective*; and the other, TabithaBrogon, LLC *that focuses on inspiring, motivating, and helping others turn their journey into meaningful experiences…*, because I truly believe, we **ALL** have something to say.

Annnd I am also an ordained Elder, and I **love** the Lord. **And I love people**. **And my *transparency* and *candor…*, that you read in this book, comes because I have finally learned how to love me too**. ***All of me!***

I HAVE SOMETHING TO SAY

With every childhood experience, the good, the bad, the 'what in the world!?!' - With every scary moment … of growing up earlier than I wanted to … of doing the best I knew how to do at that time; With every transition … every marriage … every divorce… every abuse; With every caregiver, foster parent, and family members I have gained along the way…

Today, I can look life dead in the eye,
without faking the funk,
without being
super spiritual – no, just super grateful,
Today, I can say
that
"I AM BLESSED."

God used experiences, many hands, and *my good friend, '**Strategy**'*, to shape me into who I am today. But had so much more to learn… and I will share…

In My NEXT book,

(**Yes**, I have got **more** to say, Chile!)

called:

'Don't Count me Out!'

I hope you will keep trackin' with me !

I MUST share **THE MIDDLE** of my journey with you as well! Ohhhhhhhhhhhh, I didn't get to this bed of roses looking all pretty and smelling all **Tab-u-lis-shus**, (as my best friend and dear sis says), without having to dig up **some weeds,** honey … and plow through some **funky** manure!! **LOL**

Ya gurl **repeated** some cycles that I experienced as a kid… she made some **poor** choices … **but she found Jesus** (*like He was lost*!) **LOL -** But **can I tell you**… even after finding Him, she **STILL** created some un-necessary losses! **-**

You just gonna put it out there!

YEP! - LIKE A BOSS, **I sure am!**

I DON'T HAVE TIIIIIIIIIIME TO WEAR ANY MORE MASKS, Honey!

And in my 3rd book,

(Yes, I plan to write 3!)

That book will be called,

'It's Time to Cross the Tracks'

I talk about taking the mask off. You see, I was a *Mask-wearer* for a **LONG** time! But I had to make some **better choices**. Choices that required starting off with apologies… and creating do-overs… and having transparent conversations……, and taking steps to **do** better…, and **live** better… and just **BE** better! ***And just like in this book, I think you will find humor in Books 2 and 3 as well.***

Life is a journey, and it is waaaay too short not to laugh!! Sis... Bruh...,

I feel like we are family!

And I hope that **somehow**, some **way**, the stories of my journey, **will be a blessing to <u>you</u>**, as you walk out yours!

THAT'S why I wrote this book.

I SEE YOU & I'm **<u>cheering</u>** for you!

Life is hard – but **YOU** are **a <u>BEAST</u>**!

So, keep tracking with ya gurl - for the **<u>full</u>** ride, *because as you can clearly see,* ***I <u>truly</u> have something to say!***

Oh! **... "Happily, ever after. <u>The End</u>."**

<u>I gotta keep my promise... *Google-it*, **honey!** (on Page 63)</u>

57567077R00065

Made in the USA
Columbia, SC
12 May 2019